Greece

Denise Allard

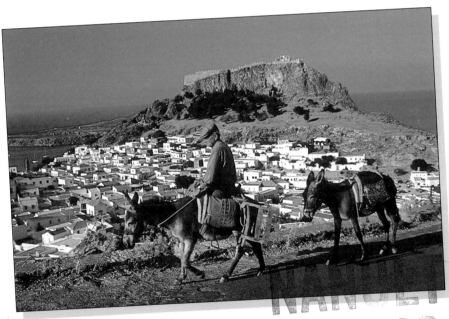

RSVP
RAINTREE
STECK-VAUGHN
P U B L I S H E R S
The Steck-Vaughn Company

Austin, Texas

Published by Raintree Steck-Vaughn Publishers, an imprint of Steck-Vaughn Company

A ZOË BOOK

Editors: Kath Davies, Pam Wells
Design: Sterling Associates
Map: Julian Baker
Production: Grahame Griffiths

Library of Congress Cataloging-in-Publication Data

Allard, Denise, 1952-
    Greece / Denise Allard.
        p. cm. — (Postcards from)
    "A Zoë Book" T.p. verso.
    Includes index.
    Summary: Short excerpts written in the form of postcards describe different places in Greece and the activities of the people who live there.
    ISBN 0-8172-4022-5 (hardcover). — ISBN 0-8172-6205-9 (softcover)
    1. Greece—Description and travel—Juvenile literature. 2. Greece—Social life and customs—20th century—Juvenile Literature. [1. Greece—Description and travel. 2. Postcards.] I. Title. II. Series.
DF728. A66 1997
949.507—dc20   95–2612
                                                                                    CIP
                                                                                     AC

Printed and bound in the United States
1 2 3 4 5 6 7 8 9 0 WZ 99 98 97 96

Photographic acknowledgments

The publishers wish to acknowledge, with thanks, the following photographic sources:

David Beatty - cover r; / Fanny Dubes - cover bl; / John Ross 10; Tony Gervis 22, 24; / Robert Harding Picture Library; Impact Photos / Mark Henley 6, 12; / John Denham 16; / Piers Cavendish 20; / Caroline Penn 26; Zefa - cover tl, title page, 8, 14, 18, 28.

The publishers have made every effort to trace the copyright holders, but if they have inadvertently overlooked any, they will be pleased to make the necessary arrangement at the first opportunity.

Contents

All the words that appear in **bold** are explained in the Glossary on page 30.

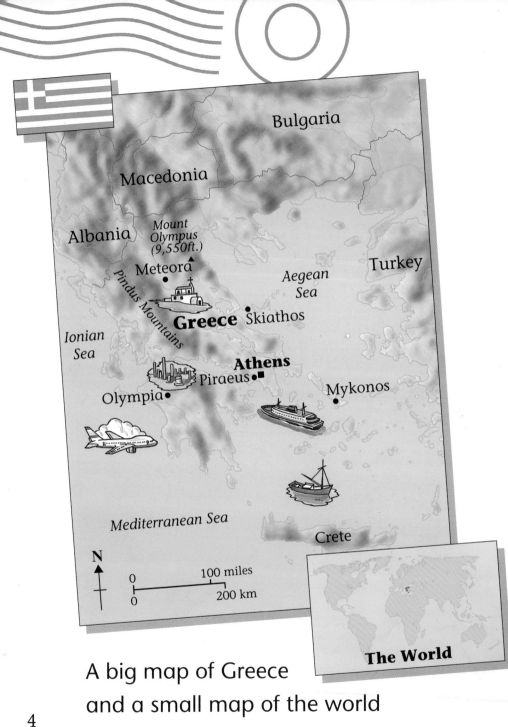

Bulgaria

Macedonia

Albania

Mount
Olympus
(9,550ft.)

Meteora

Pindus Mountains

Ionian
Sea

Greece Skiathos

Aegean
Sea

Turkey

Athens

Piraeus

Olympia

Mykonos

Mediterranean Sea

Crete

N

0   100 miles

0   200 km

The World

A big map of Greece
and a small map of the world

4

Dear Jack,

You can see Greece in red on the small map. It is in the south of Europe. The plane took about nine hours to get here from New York. The weather in Greece is hot and sunny.

Your friend,

Rob

P.S. We flew over the ocean and lots of mountains on our way here. Mom says that Greece has more than 2,000 **islands**. People do not live on many of these islands.

A bird's-eye view of Athens

Dear Diana,

Athens is the **capital** city of Greece. Many people come here to see the ancient buildings. In Athens, the streets are crowded with people and cars.

Love,

Chloe

P.S. Dad says that more than 10 million people live in Greece. At one time, many people lived in the countryside. Today, most people live in the towns by the sea.

Eating dinner at a *taverna*

Dear Maxine,

Yesterday we had lunch at a Greek **restaurant**. It was called a *taverna*. I had a big plate of fried seafood and fried potatoes. Mom paid for our meal with Greek money called *drachmas*.

Your friend,

James

P.S. Mom says that Greek people eat their main meal at midday. Sometimes people go out to eat in the evening, when it is cooler. I like Greek salads with olives and cheese.

The Parthenon in Athens

Dear Jordan,

We went to the Acropolis. It is the oldest part of Athens. The Acropolis was built on a hill about 2,500 years ago. At the top, we saw the ruins of a **temple** called the Parthenon.

Love,

Chrissy

P.S. I went to the Parthenon with my cousin, Yanni. He and his friends spoke in Greek. Yanni says that they use Greek writing at school. It is different from English writing.

A ferry leaving the island of Mykonos

Dear Bob,

We went on a big boat called a **ferry**. It took us from the busy **port** of Piraeus to the island of Mykonos. At Mykonos, the ferry picked up passengers. Then it took them back to Piraeus.

See you soon,

Ben

P.S. Mom says that many people travel between the Greek islands on small boats. On land, people often go by bus. The buses are always on time.

Shopping on Mykonos

Dear Susie,

I love staying on this island. We go to the beach every day. Then we eat at a *taverna*. The shops are full of nice things to buy. I like the clothes best.

Your friend,

Anne

P.S. You can buy all kinds of pottery here. Mom bought some dinner plates and a vase. Mom says that the Greek people were famous for making pots. Some were made more than 2,000 years ago.

Herding goats in the countryside

Dear Alex,

We are staying at a farm in the countryside. Every day the farmers go to work in the fields. We help milk the goats and collect honey from the bees.

Your friend,

Nicholas

P.S. Mom says that Greek people love to dance. You can see them in the *tavernas*. They dance to Greek music. It sounds very different from our music.

Meteora, in the mountains

Dear Fran,

We are in the mountains now. This is one of the **monasteries** of Meteora. Each one is built on top of a giant rock pillar. The **monks** had to climb a ladder to get in and out.

Yours,

Mimi

P.S. Not many people live in the mountains. We are here on a hiking vacation. Dad says that the footpaths in the mountains may not be marked. We have a map to find the way.

The Temple of Zeus at Olympia

Dear Petra,

We have come to see the ruins at Olympia. The **Olympic Games** were held here more than 2,000 years ago. We walked around the ruins of the temples and the **stadium**.

Yours,

Kim

P.S. Mom says that the Olympic Games were very important in Ancient Greece. They were part of the Greeks' religion. Every four years, people came from all over Greece to take part.

A beach on the island of Skiathos

Dear Amy,

We are having a great vacation. Today we sailed to the island of Skiathos. Lots of people come here. We swam in the warm sea. It was too hot to sit on the beach for very long.

Love,

Tim

P.S. Dad says that in the past many Greek people had to go to other countries to find work. Now they stay in Greece to work in the new hotels, restaurants, and shops.

Playing basketball at the
Olympic Stadium, Athens

Dear Rose,

My cousin Alex loves to play basketball. He follows the Greek National League. He also plays volleyball. Many of his friends like to play soccer in the evening, after school.

Your friend,

Steffi

P.S. In 1982 a new Olympic stadium opened in Athens. The Olympic Games still take place every four years. Today, different countries take turns holding the Games.

Easter in a village

Dear Philip,

It is Easter in Greece. This is an important time for **Christian** people. We watched a long **procession** move through the village. On Sunday, we ate a special Easter meal.

Your friend,

Helen

P.S. Mom says that most Greek people follow the Christian religion. Many **festivals** in Greece help people to remember Christian events.

The Greek flag

Dear Rachel,

This is the Greek flag. It has five blue stripes and four white stripes. The white cross comes from the old Greek flag. Blue and white are the colors that stand for Greece.

Love,

Brad

P.S. Mom says that Greece is a **republic**. The people of Greece choose their own leaders. This way of ruling is called a **democracy**.

Glossary

Capital: The town or city where people who rule the country meet

Christians: People who follow the teachings of Jesus. Jesus lived about 2,000 years ago.

Democracy: A country where all the people choose the leaders they want to run the country

Ferry: A large boat that carries people and cars across water

Festival: A time when people remember something special that happened in the past

Island: A piece of land that has water all around it

Monastery: A building where monks live

Monk: A man who has chosen a religious way of life. Monks live in a monastery.

Olympic Games: An important sports event that takes place every four years

Port: A town or city beside the sea. Ships come in to port to collect and deliver people or goods.

Procession: People walking together through a town or village

P.S. This stands for Post Script. A postscript is the part of a card or letter that is added at the end, after the person has signed it.

Republic: A country where the people choose their leaders. A republic does not have a king or a queen.

Restaurant: A place where people go to eat. In a restaurant, people pay for meals.

Stadium: A sports ground. There are usually rows of seats for people to watch the sports.

Temple: A building where people go to pray

Index